GALAXIES

A TRUE BOOK

by

Paul P. Sipiera

Children's Press®

A Division of Grolier Publishing

New York London Hong Kong Sydney
Danbury, Connecticut

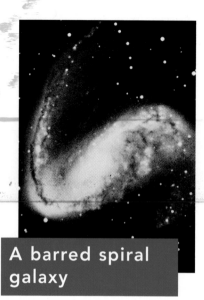

A barred spiral galaxy

Reading Consultant
Linda Cornwell
Learning Resource Consultant
Indiana Department of
Education

Science Consultant
Samuel Storch
Lecturer,
American Museum-Hayden
Planetarium, New York City

To the Adler Planetarium,
where my interest in
astronomy began,
thanks to my father

Library of Congress Cataloging-in-Publication Data

Sipiera, Paul P.
    Galaxies / by Paul Sipiera.
        p.   cm. — (A true book)
    Includes bibliographical references and index.
    Summary: Examines what a galaxy is, the different types that exist,
their structures, and some facts learned from the study of galaxies.
    ISBN 0-516-20333-9 (lib.bdg.)   0-516-26169-X (pbk.)
    1. Galaxies—Juvenile literature. [1. Galaxies.] I. Title. II. Series.
QB857.3.S57 1997
523.1'12—dc20
                                                                96-30993
                                                                CIP
                                                                AC

Contents

The Universe Around Us

The world around us looks like a very big place. Great oceans divide the continents and huge mountains touch the sky.

As seen from space, however, the world looks different. It takes astronauts in the Space Shuttle just about 11 minutes to pass over the

A view of Earth from a spacecraft (left) and a more distant view of Earth from space (right)

entire United States. From the Moon, the Earth looks like a little blue marble in space. The farther we travel from Earth, the smaller it looks.

When we look up into the night sky, we see hundreds of

stars. Each of these stars is much like our Sun. Some are bigger and some are smaller, but they are all very far from Earth. If we lived on a planet orbiting one of these stars, our Sun would be just a point of light in the sky.

A view of Earth from the Moon

A Band of Light

Ancient astronomers knew the stars well. Often, they wondered about the bright band of light that crossed the night sky. To the Greeks, it was known as the "milky circle." The Romans named it the "milky road," or the Milky Way, as it is called today.

The billions of stars that make up our galaxy (top left) look much the same today as they did to 13th-century astronomers (left) and to Galileo (top right) in the 1600s.

In the past, the Milky Way was a great mystery. No one really knew what it was. Then, in 1610, Italian astronomer Galileo discovered the truth.

With his small telescope, he saw that the band of light was really billions of distant stars.

Years later, astronomers realized that the Milky Way had a spiral shape as seen from the inside out. Today, astronomers know that the Milky Way is a huge group of stars called a galaxy. At one time, people thought the Milky Way was the entire universe. That idea would later change, too.

A Galaxy of Stars

All the stars we see at night belong to the Milky Way galaxy. A galaxy consists of a huge number of stars that move around a common center of gravity. This center is called the nucleus. Here, billions of stars are close enough to each other to

The center of a galaxy is called the nucleus (left). The center of the Milky Way is in the constellation of Sagittarius (right).

appear to be a single bright core. As seen from Earth, the center of our galaxy lies in the direction of the constellation of Sagittarius.

The Sun is one of more than 200 billion stars in the Milky Way. And our galaxy is not alone in space. There may be over 100 billion other galaxies in the universe. The universe is all created things—from the largest galaxy to the smallest atom.

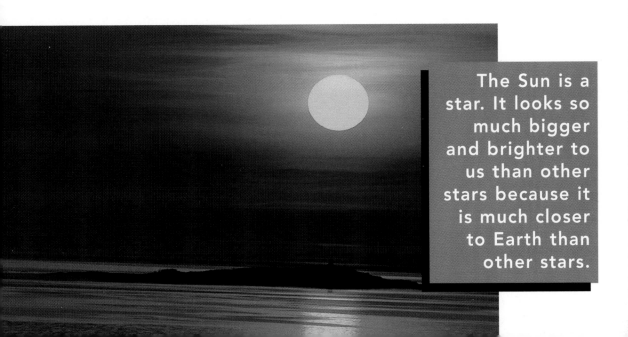

The Sun is a star. It looks so much bigger and brighter to us than other stars because it is much closer to Earth than other stars.

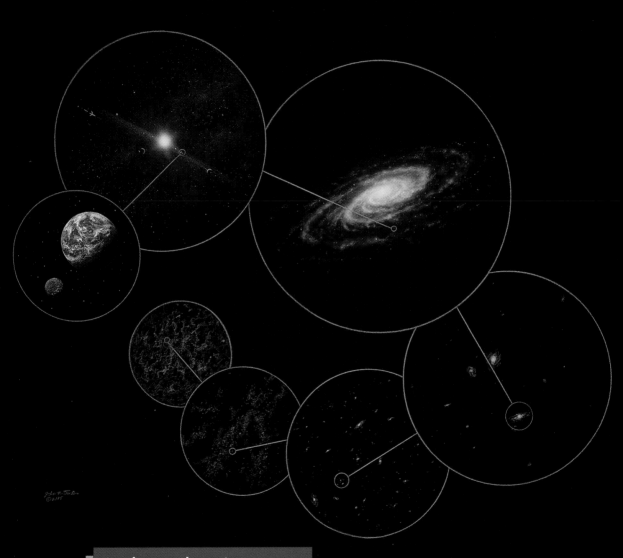

A chart showing our place in the universe

Galaxies are not evenly spread out across space. If we could see the universe all at once, we would see ribbons of galaxies stretching out in all directions. Each galaxy contains billions of stars.

Empty space lies between the galaxies. Most galaxies are clustered into groups, both large and small. Between the groups there is only the blackness of space. The universe might look something like a piece of Swiss cheese!

The Shapes of Galaxies

Galaxies come in many different shapes. They have been classified by shape into three basic types. These are elliptical, spiral, and irregularly shaped galaxies.

Elliptical galaxies are the most common, but are the hardest to see. They are usually small and dim compared to spirals. They range in shape from oval to almost round. Old, red stars populate elliptical galaxies. There is very little gas and dust present to form new stars.

A spiral galaxy has a pinwheel shape. Viewed from the side, it looks like a flattened disk with a bulge in the middle. It contains both old, red stars and young, blue stars. Dense regions of gas and dust can be seen along the edge of its disk.

Our Milky Way galaxy is believed to be a spiral. We cannot be sure of its exact shape, because we are inside it. To really see its shape, we would have to travel to a nearby galaxy and look back.

An illustration of a spiral galaxy (top), and a spiral galaxy viewed from the side (bottom)

This is a false-color image of an irregular galaxy (top). The Small Magellanic Cloud (middle) and the Large Magellanic Cloud (bottom) are irregular galaxies.

The last group is called the irregulars. These galaxies have large amounts of gas and dust with many blue stars, like the spirals. The difference is that irregular galaxies have no real shape.

Two of the closest galaxies to the Milky Way are irregulars. These galaxies are called the Magellanic Clouds. Both can be seen from the Earth's southern hemisphere. They are so close you don't even need a telescope to see them.

The Structure of a Spiral Galaxy

A typical spiral galaxy has three main parts. The center is called the nucleus. Here, a large number of old red stars are packed closely together. Surrounding the nucleus is the disk, which includes the arms. The disk is the brightest part

Old red stars are packed together in the nucleus of a spiral galaxy. Younger, blue stars are found along the arms of the spirals.

of the galaxy. Large amounts of gas and dust are found in the arms. This is where new stars are born. A halo of stars and a number of globular clusters surround the entire galaxy.

Spiral galaxies are further divided into three groups by their different shapes. The first is an SO type spiral. It has no spiral arms, only a few young stars, and little gas and dust. But it is still called a spiral because of its bright disk.

The second group of spirals are classified into Sa, Sb, and Sc groups. These galaxies range from tight bright disks to very open pinwheels. Each galaxy is classified by how

Galaxy M104 (top), also known as the Sombrero galaxy, is an Sa-type spiral galaxy. An Sb-type spiral galaxy (left) is more tightly coiled than an Sc-type spiral galaxy (right).

tightly its arms are coiled around its nucleus. These are referred to as normal spirals.

A barred
spiral galaxy

The third type is a barred spiral. It looks very different from a normal spiral. It has a smaller nucleus of stars with a barlike structure running through it. Its arms extend out from the ends of the bar.

Unusual Galaxies

Most galaxies appear to be rather quiet. A few galaxies give off violent bursts of energy or flares of matter that shoot off into space. The great M87 elliptical galaxy is one of these. Recent studies of M87 indicate that a giant black hole may be the cause

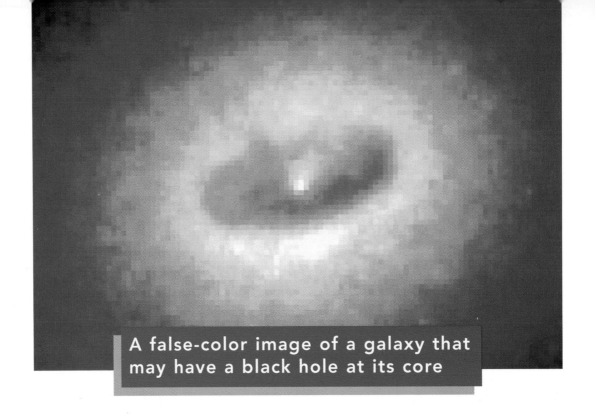

A false-color image of a galaxy that may have a black hole at its core

of this huge eruption of matter and energy. A black hole is an object formed from the death of a very large star. Its gravity is so strong that even light does not travel fast enough to escape.

Galaxy M87

The largest known galaxy is an elliptical galaxy called M87. It has more than 5 trillion stars, and may even have a giant black hole at its center.

Although the distances between galaxies are great, sometimes they collide. When this happens, a galaxy's shape can be changed.

Even if two galaxies do not actually collide, a close pass may have a lasting effect. This is true for our Milky Way and the two smaller galaxies called the Magellanic Clouds. It appears that 200 million years ago, the Magellanic Clouds passed through the outer edge

of the Milky Way. This caused a
long "bridge" of gas to form
between each of them.

In time, it is believed that
the two smaller galaxies will
join the Milky Way and form
one giant galaxy.

The Importance of Galaxies

The position of a galaxy in the universe can help astronomers measure the size of the universe. Measuring the distance to a galaxy is not easy. Astronomers often estimate the distance to a galaxy by using different

This galaxy, NGC 6822, is one of the nearest galaxies to us—it's only about 2 million light-years away. It is so close that many of its individual stars can be seen.

experiments in physics. This helps give astronomers an idea of how big and old the universe really is.

This spiral galaxy (top), about 10 million light-years away, is seen almost edge-on as viewed from Earth. The special photo on the bottom, taken by the Hubble Space Telescope, shows the core of the most-distant known galaxy. This galaxy is about 14 billion light-years away.

The distances to other galaxies are so large that they cannot be measured in kilometers or miles. Instead, astronomers measure large distances in space in units called light-years. One light-year is the distance light travels through space in one year. It adds up to almost 6 trillion miles (more than 9 trillion km). Our Milky Way galaxy measures about 100,000 light-years across. The farthest galaxy from Earth that we know of is about 14 billion light-years away.

The arrow in this photograph points to the most-distant known galaxy.

Seeing a distant galaxy is like looking back in time. Each time astronomers discover a galaxy farther away than any other, it means that the universe is even older than previously thought. That is because the light from that galaxy had to travel millions of light-years to reach us. If, for example, a galaxy is found to be 12 billion light-years away, than the universe must be at least 12 billion years old, since that amount of time would be required for the light from the galaxy to reach us. When we look at a distant galaxy, we see it as it was long ago, and not how it looks today.

You'd Have to Live to Be 100,000 Years Old!

Traveling at the speed of light, it would take a traveler 100,000 years to cross the Milky Way galaxy from edge to edge.

100,000 light-years

An illustration of how our galaxy might look if viewed edge on

One of the few objects we can see in the night sky that is not part of the Milky Way is the Andromeda galaxy. It is a giant spiral galaxy that is somewhat larger than the Milky Way. It is more than 2.2 million light-years from Earth.

On a clear, moonless night in an area away from city lights, this galaxy appears as a dim smudge of light in the constellation of Andromeda.

The Andromeda galaxy, as it appears when viewed through a powerful telescope

If you can see it, you are looking beyond the stars of our galaxy and out into distant space. The Andromeda galaxy is as far as the eye can see without using a telescope.

How galaxies form is an important question that astronomers try to answer. Many astronomers believe that galaxies formed more than 12 billion years ago, as gases from the Big Bang were drawn together by gravity. Before that, there may have been no stars at all. Keep in mind that galaxies are made up of billions of individual stars. Astronomers believe that galaxies formed like stars do, only on a much larger scale.

The study of other galaxies presents scientists with many difficult problems. Because we see galaxies as they looked long ago, and galaxies change with time, a distant galaxy may actually be quite different from what we see in our telescopes. Some of the most distant galaxies may have died out billions of years ago. We can only look through our telescopes and wonder. In studying galaxies,

A cluster of galaxies

astronomers can look back
in time and see what the
universe was like when it
was young.

To Find Out More

Here are some additional resources to help you learn more about galaxies:

 **Books**

Couper, Heather and Henbest, Nigel, **Astronomy.** Franklin Watts, 1983.

Darling, David J., **The Galaxies: Cities of Stars.** Dillon Press, 1985.

Dolan, Terrance, **Probing Deep Space.** Chelsea House Ridge Press Book, 1975.

Engelbrektson, June, **Stars, Planets and Galaxies.** Ridge Press Book, 1975.

Ferris, Timothy, **Galaxies.** Sierra Club, 1980.

Knight, David C., **Galaxies.** William Morrow and Company, 1979.

Lippincott, Kristen, **Astronomy.** Dorling Kindersley Publishing, Inc., 1994.

Simon, Seymour, **Galaxies.** Morrow Junior Books, 1985.

Sipiera, Diane M. and Sipiera, Paul P., **Constellations.** Children's Press, 1997.

Organizations

Astronomical Society of the Pacific
1290 24th Avenue
San Francisco, CA 94122
http://www.physics.sfsu.edu/asp

Junior Astronomical Society
58 Vaughan Gardens
Ilford Essex IG1 3PD
England

The Planetary Society
5 North Catalina Avenue
Pasadena, CA 91106
e-mail: *tps.lc@genie.geis.com*

Online Sites

The Planetary Studies Foundation
http://homepage.interaccess.com/~jpatpsf/>.

Galaxy Features On-Line!
http://hou.161.gov/galaxyfeaturesonline.html

Important Words

astronomer scientist who studies stars, planets, and the other objects that make up the universe

black hole object formed from the death of a very large star; its gravity is so strong that even light does not travel fast enough to escape

constellation group of stars made to represent the image of a person or object in the sky

globular cluster "ball" of very old red stars found above and below the disk of the Milky Way galaxy

gravity the force of attraction between two objects; it is what keeps you from falling off the Earth into space

planet smaller body of rock or gas that orbits a star; it does not give off light like a star

Index

Meet the Author

Paul P. Sipiera is a professor of geology and astronomy at William Rainey Harper College in Palatine, Illinois. His main area of research is meteorites. When he is not studying science, he can be found working on his farm in Galena, Illinois, with his wife, Diane, and their three daughters, Andrea, Paula Frances, and Carrie Ann.